STATE OF VER[MONT]
DEPARTMENT OF L[IBRARIES]
NORTHWEST REGIONA[L]
RFD #2
FAIRFAX, VERMONT

WITHDRAWN

VERMONT DEPARTMENT OF LIBRARIES
MIDSTATE REGIONAL LIBRARY
RR #4, BOX 1870
MONTPELIER, VERMONT 05602

 Country Music Library

The Grand Ole Opry

ROBERT K. KRISHEF

 Lerner Publications Company ▪ Minneapolis

ACKNOWLEDGMENTS: The illustrations are reproduced through the courtesy of: pp. 4, 6, 19, 20, 22, 24, 27, 34, 37, 46, 66, Country Music Association Library and Media Center; p. 8, WSB Radio; pp. 11, 32, 51, 54, 56, 58, 61, Opryland Public Relations; pp. 12, 60, Department of Tourist Development, State of Tennessee; p. 17, Les Leverett; p. 29, National Life and Accident Insurance Company; p. 41, Top Billing; pp. 44, 45, 71, Board of Directors of the Country Music Association, Inc.

Front cover photo: Opryland Public Relations

LIBRARY OF CONGRESS CATALOGING IN PUBLICATION DATA

Krishef, Robert K.
Grand Ole Opry.

(Country Music Library)
Includes index.
SUMMARY: A history of the Grand Ole Opry discussing its beginnings, various locations, stars, and growth into today's Opryland entertainment park in Nashville.

1. Grand Ole Opry (Radio programs) — Juvenile literature.
[1. Grand Ole Opry (Radio program). 2. Country music.] I. Title.
ML3930.G72K74   784   77-90151
ISBN 0-8225-1405-2

DISCARDED

Copyright © 1978 by Lerner Publications Company

All rights reserved. International copyright secured. No part of this book may be reproduced in any form whatsoever without permission in writing from the publisher except for the inclusion of brief quotations in an acknowledged review.

Manufactured in the United States of America. Published simultaneously in Canada by J. M. Dent & Sons (Canada) Ltd., Don Mills, Ontario.

International Standard Book Number: 0-8225-1405-2
Library of Congress Catalog Card Number: 77-90151

1 2 3 4 5 6 7 8 9 10 85 84 83 82 81 80 79 78

Contents

	Introduction	5
1	The Beginning	9
2	The Birth of the Opry	15
3	An Institution Develops	25
4	The Star System	35
5	Home at the Ryman	47
6	The Opry Today	57
7	Opry Tradition	67
	Index	72

Live entertainment at the Grand Ole Opry

Introduction

When people think of country music, they think of the Grand Ole Opry. First broadcast as the WSM Barn Dance on November 28, 1925, in Nashville, Tennessee, the Opry is today the oldest radio and stage show in history. Because of the Opry's enduring popularity, Nashville has become the country music capital of the world and has been given the nickname "Music City, U.S.A." Regular Saturday night broadcasts still originate from Nashville through station WSM.

The Nashville Chamber of Commerce has estimated that the city's music industry is a billion-dollar-a-year business. This estimate is based on the total sales volume of the city's recording studios, recording companies, publishing houses, talent agencies, and other music-related firms. The billion-dollar estimate includes the tourist industry as well. Each year, about 750,000 people visit the Opry. These visitors come from every state in the Union and travel an average of nearly 1,000 miles round trip.

The number of people who listen to the Opry broadcast every Saturday night, however, is even greater than the number who visit. Every week,

WSM's radio tower was at one time America's tallest.

over a million people listen to the program. For many of them, listening to the Grand Ole Opry is a tradition of many years' standing. Even sponsors are devoted to the show. Some sponsors have been with the Opry for more than 30 years.

The Opry is a program that defies normal show business procedure. Officials do not know more than 48 hours in advance who is going to be on the show. So there is no advance promotion of artists, and there are no rehearsals. Still, the Grand Ole Opry thrives, and people like it. Growth has come because of the show's informality, rather than in spite of it. People may not know who they are going to see at the Opry after they have traveled hundreds of miles to get there. But they do know that they are going to see a good show.

The story of the Grand Ole Opry is the story of an organization that puts on a good show and that gives its audiences the kind of music they love. It is a fascinating chapter in the history of country music.

James and Martha Carson, the "Barn Dance Sweethearts" of Radio WSB in Atlanta, Georgia. In 1922, WSB became the first station to broadcast country music.

The Beginning 1

The Grand Ole Opry started as a barn dance, a musical program that featured genuine country folk tunes. Since many radio stations founded in the 1920s and 1930s had barn dance programs, the Opry was not unique. But it was the only barn dance program to last.

Before radio, country music was enjoyed only at rural social events. When country music came to radio, however, country music fans could hear their favorite music whenever they wanted to. Record companies, of course, had been in existence since the turn of the century. But country music artists — or "hillbilly" singers, as they were called — were not being recorded. This was because the record companies did not recognize or appreciate the wide popularity of country music.

The record companies realized their mistake when country music started to be broadcast on radio. Sales of radio sets rose dramatically, while sales of records declined. So record companies sent talent scouts out to find and record country musicians. The musicians that they found quickly discovered that making records helped them get better radio jobs, and that their radio exposure helped sell their records. It was radio and records — which sometimes helped one another and sometimes competed — that led to the creation of the country music industry.

The first radio station to broadcast country music was WSB in Atlanta, Georgia, in 1922. In 1923, station WBAP in Fort Worth, Texas, began a program of country, or hillbilly, dance music. In Chicago, Illinois, station WLS started a barn dance program in 1924. This program attained immediate national recognition and eventually became the famous National Barn Dance.

In Nashville, Tennessee, these developments were viewed with interest by an insurance executive named Edwin W. Craig. Craig was vice-president of the National Life and Accident Insurance Company. His father, C. A. Craig, was president of the company and one of its owners. Edwin Craig's business was insurance, but his hobby was radio. An enthusiastic ham radio operator, Craig was convinced that the radio industry had a bright future. He also happened to be an amateur musician who played the mandolin and enjoyed hillbilly music.

Edwin Craig, the guiding force behind the creation of Radio WSM and the Grand Ole Opry

Because of his interests, Craig came to believe that ownership of a country music radio station would be a good investment for the National Life and Accident Insurance Company. He tried to persuade company owners to apply for a radio license, but found that they were not very enthusiastic. What, they wondered, did radio have to do with selling insurance? They also worried that Nashville was an unlikely place to locate a country music radio station.

This view stemmed from the cultural differences that existed between Nashville and the rural areas in the 1920s. Rural communities reflected the hard life, simple tastes, and earthy music of its people. Nashville, on the other hand, was a sophisticated city that called itself the "Athens of the South." This self-image was reflected in such things as Nashville's many colleges and universities and its full-sized replica of the Parthenon, an ancient temple in Athens, Greece. The city also proudly

Nashville's replica of the Parthenon

claimed three United States Presidents as one-time residents — Andrew Jackson, Andrew Johnson, and James Polk. In the area of music and drama, Nashville had played host to such world-famous artists as the celebrated Polish pianist Paderewski, violinist Fritz Kreisler, singer Enrico Caruso, actresses Sarah Bernhardt and Helen Hayes, and others.

In spite of the differences that separated Nashville from the rural areas, Craig continued his efforts to establish a country music station in the "Athens of the South." He knew that country music was a vital force in America's musical heritage. He reasoned that even if there weren't many listeners in Nashville, there would be large country music audiences in the rural areas. As Craig pointed out to the insurance company owners, the residents of these rural communities were called on regularly by National's insurance agents. Wouldn't they feel something in common with the agents if the National Life and Accident Insurance Company owned a country music radio station? And if so, wouldn't this help insurance sales?

That argument, no doubt, was the clincher, for Craig eventually got permission to go ahead with plans for a radio station. One of his first promotional moves was to obtain the call letters WSM for the station. These letters represented the first letter of each word in the company's slogan, "We Shield Millions."

On October 5, 1925, WSM went on the air. At the controls was a young man named John H. ("Jack") DeWitt, Jr., a pioneer in the building of radio equipment who later became president of WSM. Edwin Craig officially opened the station with the words "This is WSM, we shield millions, the National Life and Accident Insurance Company of Nashville, Tennessee." Then his father, C. A. Craig, dedicated WSM "to the public service."

Others in attendance at the dedication ceremony included Tennessee Governor Austin Peay, Nashville Mayor Hilary Howse, and several noted radio announcers. One of the visiting radio personalities was the announcer of the WLS Barn Dance in Chicago. This man had just been voted "most popular announcer in the United States" in a poll conducted by *Radio Digest* magazine. His name was George Dewey Hay.

The Birth of the Opry 2

After WSM was launched, Edwin Craig looked for a special kind of personality to direct the station. He wanted someone well known — if possible — to bring prestige to WSM and to the National Life and Accident Insurance Company. This person had to be distinctive and imaginative, and his philosophy of programming had to be right for country music radio.

Craig found the man he was looking for in George D. Hay. As announcer of the popular WLS Barn Dance, Hay was well known. He had a way with words, and he knew how to do things in a way that would capture people's attention. A fun-loving person, Hay had a comical nickname for himself — the "Solemn Old Judge." This nickname was amusing because Hay was only 29 years old, he was not solemn, and he was certainly not a judge.

Hay had gotten his start in radio when the newspaper he was working for, the Memphis, Tennessee, *Commercial Appeal,* started radio station WMC in Memphis. Hay worked as radio editor for the newspaper and gradually moved into broadcasting at WMC. There, he started the announcing gimmick that became his trademark — blowing a steamboat whistle to signal the beginning and end of each show.

In 1924, Hay became chief announcer for WLS radio's National Barn Dance in Chicago. Due to the show's large listening audience, Hay became one of the best known radio announcers in the country. Then, in October 1925, Hay traveled to Nashville for the dedication of radio station WSM. He met Edwin Craig and found that they shared similar beliefs about country music radio. Both deeply admired country music and felt that it was entitled to recognition on the American music scene. Both also believed that a country radio station should play only authentic country folk tunes — music that was "close to the ground," in Hay's words.

On the basis of these and other shared beliefs, George Hay was hired to direct station WSM. As director, Hay was responsible for planning the format of the program. He decided to create a regular barn dance program much like the WLS National Barn Dance. While looking for talented musicians, Hay met an 80-year-old fiddler named

Uncle Jimmy Thompson, who boasted that he could "fiddle the taters off the vine." Hay decided that Thompson would be ideal for the first show.

At 8:00 P.M., Saturday, November 28, 1925, the WSM Barn Dance went on the air. The station director introduced himself as the Solemn Old Judge and invited listeners to send telegrams requesting songs. Then he turned the microphone over to Thompson, who was waiting expectantly in a cushioned chair, fiddle over his knee. Thompson

Judge Hay and Uncle Jimmy Thompson at the first Opry broadcast

played a few tunes, and then the telegrams began arriving. Uncle Jimmy fiddled steadily for an hour, accompanied on the piano by his niece, Eva Thompson Jones. When Judge Hay blew his steamboat whistle to signal the end of the program, Uncle Jimmy wasn't very pleased. "Why shucks," he complained, "a man don't get warmed up in an hour. I just won an eight-day fiddling contest down in Dallas."

The new WSM radio program was a hit. And Hay knew how to keep the interest alive. To drum up publicity, Hay set up a fiddling competition. He challenged a fiddling champion from Maine, Mellie Dunham, to a contest with Uncle Jimmy Thompson, and advertised it in the newspapers. Dunham, however, refused the challenge. The refusal aroused a feeling of pride in the listeners and earned some prestige for the radio station. "He's afeared of me," Uncle Jimmy would declare on the air.

Public interest in the radio show grew so much that listeners began showing up at the radio station on Saturday nights. The studio was too small to accommodate everyone, so the visitors had to watch the broadcast from outside, through large glass windows. People who took a special interest in the new program were the local country musicians. They flocked to the station when they heard that Judge Hay was going to hold auditions for local

The Crook Brothers were among the many local Nashville acts that performed regularly at the Opry.

talent. The auditions yielded a lot of promising performers for WSM. Before long, Uncle Jimmy Thompson was overshadowed by other featured acts, including Sam and Kirk McGee, the Crook Brothers, and Uncle Ed Poplin and his Ole Timers.

Many of the bands that appeared on the show had particularly colorful hillbilly names, such as the Gully Jumpers or the Fruit Jar Drinkers. If a band didn't have an appropriate name, Hay could think of one. When Dr. Humphrey Bate and his group performed on the WSM Barn Dance, the Judge named the group the Possum Hunters.

In 1926, almost a year after its start, the WSM Barn Dance got its first star. He was 55-year-old Uncle Dave Macon, a high-kicking banjoist, singer, and humorous storyteller who was known as the "Dixie Dewdrop." Macon's exposure over WSM eventually made him a legend in country music. And he, in turn, helped increase the Barn Dance's popularity. Part of Macon's success was due to the

Uncle Dave Macon, the first Opry "star"

good working relationship he had with Judge Hay. In spite of the age difference between them, the two men had a long and profitable association. Opry historians say that Uncle Dave admired Hay's "inquiring mind, friendliness, and command of the language," while Hay appreciated the older man's "deep religious beliefs, showmanship, and talent."

By 1927, the WSM Barn Dance had become a three-hour program and a Saturday night tradition for its ever-increasing audience. Even so, there were other good barn dance programs on the radio, and each had talented musicians and popular personalities as well. Something happened at WSM, however, that made its program more recognizable and more memorable than any of the others.

The radio program scheduled before the WSM Barn Dance was a network program of a completely different kind. This program was the Musical Appreciation Hour, featuring the New York Symphony Orchestra conducted by Dr. Walter Damrosch. One evening, Dr. Damrosch presented as his last selection a new composition that included the musical sound of a speeding locomotive coming to a puffing stop. Dr. Damrosch explained that such realism was unusual for a symphony composition. "I am breaking a rule," he said in a refined voice, "because most artists realize there is no place in the classics for realism."

Judge Hay backstage at the Opry

Judge Hay, who had been listening, felt that the comment was a "put down" of country music — a music form that was *based* on realism. When he went on the air with the Barn Dance, Hay responded to Dr. Damrosch's seemingly superior tone. "Dr. Damrosch told us . . . that there is no place in the classics for realism. But from here on out, we will present nothing but realism. It will be down to earth for the earthy."

Then Hay presented a WSM performer named DeFord Bailey, a young black who was an expert on the harmonica. Bailey played a country version of "Pan American Blues," another train song. The song, Hay said, was "in respectful contrast to Dr. Damrosch's number, which depicts the onrush of locomotives."

When Bailey had finished, Judge Hay took the microphone again. His next remark caught the imagination of the country music world, and gave the WSM Barn Dance one of the most descriptive titles in the history of radio.

"For the past hour," he said, "we have been listening to music taken largely from grand opera, but from now on we will present the Grand Ole Opry."

Radio WSM's first recording studio

An Institution Develops 3

The Grand Ole Opry did not succeed just because of its name. The name, however, did provide a dramatic and appealing title for the program. It was a natural. Listeners liked it and felt comfortable with it. Letters began arriving from fans who, in the process of requesting songs or making other comments, referred almost matter-of-factly to the show as the Grand Ole Opry. It was almost as though George Hay had *intended* to change the show's name, for that is the effect his remark had. Soon, the show officially became known as the Grand Ole Opry.

The new name, combined with other factors, helped propel the Opry to national fame. Among these factors were the improved quality of entertainment at the Opry, the emergence of the Opry as a stage show, the addition of important behind-the-scenes personnel, and the steady development and prosperity of station WSM.

In 1932, WSM received permission from the Federal Radio Commission (today the Federal Communications Commission) to increase the power and range of its radio signal. This enabled the station to increase its daytime power from 5,000 watts to 50,000 watts and to have a clear channel frequency at night. ("Clear channel" meant that no other station could operate on WSM's frequency.) As a result, millions of new listeners could hear the Grand Ole Opry and other WSM programs simply by turning their radio dials to 650.

As the Opry grew, it became known as a place where country musicians could display their talents and boost their careers. Years before, during the early 1920s, most country musicians did not think of music as a career. To them, music was a hobby, something they did in their leisure time. As storekeepers, farmers, or professional people, they played for the love of their hobby and not for the money. Dr. Humphrey Bate, for example, was a medical doctor who liked to play harmonica in his spare time.

By the late 1920s and early 1930s, however, acts were beginning to appear that were more polished and professional than the early acts. These performers hoped to earn a living, or at least a partial living, from their music. As a result, the Opry started building a regular cast of performers who were paid. The acts included string bands like the

Dixieliners, Jack Shook and the Missouri Mountaineers, Zeke Clements and the Bronco Busters, and also fiddlers such as Curley Fox.

Most of the music on the Opry was instrumental, even though performers like Uncle Dave Macon did sing from time to time. But new additions to the cast included performers who were known more as singers than as instrumentalists. These included Asher Sizemore and his son, "Little Jimmy" Sizemore, an act that was often at the Opry

The Dixieliners

during the early 1930s. A highly professional trio named the Vagabonds joined the Opry at about this time, and so did the Delmore Brothers and Robert Lunn, a "talking blues" entertainer.

More comedy was also added to Opry acts, although some entertainers had always included comedy in their acts. Zeke Clements was one of the early comedians on the Grand Ole Opry. And one of the early comedy teams consisted of two women, "Sarie and Sally" (Edna Wilson and Margaret Waters), who told stories in rural dialect.

The rapid growth of the Grand Ole Opry was definitely a surprise to the founder of WSM, Edwin Craig. He knew that country music was popular. But he had not expected the Opry to become so large in terms of numbers of performers. (By 1930, there were more than 30 people in the cast.) Nor had he guessed that so many listeners would want to see the Opry in person.

Noting the acceptance of the Grand Ole Opry, Craig expanded the Opry radio broadcast into a stage show presentation. The first thing he did was to have a 500-seat studio built in the National Life and Accident Insurance Company building. Unfortunately — or perhaps fortunately, as it turned out — 500 seats were not nearly enough to accommodate all the people who wanted to see the Opry. Before one Saturday evening performance, the area outside the front of the building was so

The National Life and Accident Insurance Company building in Nashville, 1925

crowded that some National Life executives could not get into their own offices. This made the executives so angry that they refused to let the Opry have an audience at the broadcast.

Opry officials were upset over this, for they had found that a live audience contributed much to the excitement and enjoyment of their program. Unwilling to accept the executives' decision, Opry officials decided to move. They rented a former movie house, the Hillsboro Theater, and held two shows there on Saturday nights. Admission was free, but it was by ticket only. Since most of the tickets were obtained through agents of National Life, some insurance was probably purchased as well. As Craig had originally anticipated, owning a country music station was a profitable venture for the insurance company.

In time, the Hillsboro Theater also became too small. In 1936, the Opry moved to the Dixie Tabernacle, a former revival house. The bench seats were full of splinters and there was sawdust on the floor, but the building could seat almost 3,000 people. In 1939, another move was made to an even larger building, the newly constructed War Memorial Auditorium. Here, the Grand Ole Opry charged admission for the first time — 25 cents.

The Opry's growth in the 1930s brought growing pains, stress that resulted in certain changes in the organization. Back in 1925, Edwin Craig had hired George Hay to manage WSM. Now, almost 10 years later, Hay did not have the time to handle the business affairs of a rapidly growing radio station. So a new station manager, Harry Stone, was hired. As the Opry grew, however, it became apparent to Stone that Hay was having difficulty managing it. Stone then decided to free Hay from his duties backstage so that he could concentrate on what he did best — act as announcer and master of ceremonies for the show.

In 1934 Vito Pellettieri, a one-time classical violinist and orchestra leader, was appointed stage manager of the Grand Ole Opry. For years, Pellettieri had been music librarian at WSM. As music librarian, he was respected for his knowledge of music, of composers, and of music publishers. At first, Pellettieri refused the new assignment with the Opry. "I don't know anything about those hillbillies," he stormed to Harry Stone, "and I don't want anything to do with that show!"

Pellettieri finally accepted the assignment. But after spending one Saturday evening at the Hillsboro Theater, he was more certain than ever that he didn't want to have anything to do with the show. Informality had gotten out of hand at the Grand Ole Opry. Performers came when they felt like it, and left when they felt like it. And some who were scheduled to be on the program didn't appear at all. The following Monday morning, Vito complained to Stone, who listened patiently and then replied, "I told you to run the show any way you wanted to. Just don't bother me with your problems. Do it your way."

After that, Vito Pellettieri did do it his way. He met with each act and told the members that if they were not at the theater when they were supposed to be, they needn't come back at all, for they were through. The crackdown did not cost the Opry its informal, spontaneous quality. But it did make

Vito Pellettieri was stage manager of the Opry for many years.

clear who the boss was and what he expected.

Vito Pellettieri's professionalism and WSM's strong clear-channel signal helped make the Grand Ole Opry more popular than ever in the 1930s. And people throughout the United States were steadily becoming familiar with Opry stars because of the Artists' Service Bureau, which promoted Opry acts in every part of the country. Because of its expanded coverage, the Opry became even more attractive to advertisers who wanted to reach a lot of people. Crystal Water Crystals, manufacturers of an all-purpose medicine, became the show's first sponsor in 1934, followed by Stephens Work Clothes and Martha White Flour Mills. The last two companies still advertise on the Opry today.

Among those who followed the progress of WSM and the Opry were the executives of the National Broadcasting Company (NBC). WSM had been affiliated with the NBC network since 1927. In the 1930s, the Nashville station produced many live shows for NBC, which fed these shows to other stations around the country. The supervisor for many of these live shows was Jack Stapp, a man of considerable experience who had worked in New York. He was program manager at WSM and second in command to Harry Stone.

The quality of Stapp's programs convinced NBC officials that WSM was capable of making the Grand Ole Opry a successful network program. In 1939, WSM got a large national sponsor for the Opry. It was the R. J. Reynolds Company, which bought a half-hour of the program to advertise its Prince Albert Tobacco. This half-hour was put on the network.

In 1940, Hollywood beckoned. Republic Pictures made a movie called, appropriately enough, *Grand Ole Opry*. The combination of a nationally distributed motion picture and nationwide radio exposure through NBC clinched the Opry's reputation in its field. It was, at last, recognized as a leading institution of country music.

Roy Acuff, singing star of the Opry

The Star System 4

Among the Opry people featured in the movie *Grand Ole Opry* were Judge George Hay, Uncle Dave Macon, and Roy Acuff. Acuff was a young singer whose mushrooming career was starting a new trend at the Opry.

Until Roy Acuff came along, the Opry featured mostly instrumental music. Performers like Uncle Dave Macon did sing, but they were not known primarily for their singing. Others specialized in singing, but their acts were never the most important parts of the program. Acuff, however, was the first singing star of the Opry, and the first to become as well known nationally as the program itself.

Acuff appeared at the Opry for the first time in 1937. He had a powerful voice, and he projected it vigorously. Even though radio microphones and audio equipment were not very advanced in those days, no one had any trouble hearing *his* lyrics. This was a vast improvement over other singers who were more soft-spoken and therefore hard to understand. Listeners especially liked Acuff's sincerity. He was known for actually crying on stage when he sang a sad song.

In 1938 Roy and his band, the Crazy Tennesseans, joined the regular cast of the Grand Ole Opry. The name of the band soon came up for discussion, however. Harry Stone and Judge Hay thought that the name might offend people. So at Hay's suggestion, the band was renamed the Smoky Mountain Boys. It was an indication that times were changing and that the Opry was becoming more conscious of its image.

By the early 1940s, Acuff had become an institution in show business and was earning hundreds of thousands of dollars a year. His records, which included "The Great Speckled Bird" and "Wabash Cannonball," sold in the millions. In addition to his singing career, Acuff and songwriter Fred Rose started Acuff-Rose Publications, the first music publishing company to specialize in country music. Rose provided the musical knowledge and Acuff provided the money. One story has it that shortly after Fred Rose told his new partner how much cash they needed to get started, Roy Acuff appeared with the required amount — thousands of dollars — in a paper sack!

Following Acuff's rise to stardom, other country music artists established their professional reputations at the Opry, too. Ernest Tubb joined the Opry in 1943 after recording his hit song "I'm Walking the Floor over You." He became one of the most famous "honky tonk" singers of his day. Honky tonks were noisy dance halls and bars, and the music played there had a heavier beat than other kinds of country music.

Roy Acuff (left) *and Ernest Tubb*

Eddy Arnold rose from the featured vocalist spot with Pee Wee King and the Golden West Cowboys to featured performer on the Opry. He succeeded Acuff in the middle and late 1940s as the leading recording artist in country music. Red Foley was another Opry singing star of this period. Both he and Arnold had smoother voices than Acuff and Tubb.

Other performers also introduced unique sounds to the Grand Ole Opry. In 1939, a Kentucky-born mandolin player and singer, Bill Monroe, was hired as a regular on the show. At the time, there was no particular name for his hard-driving, high-pitched music. But eventually it became known as "bluegrass." Lester Flatt, Earl Scruggs, and many other bluegrass musicians were, at one time or another, members of Monroe's band.

Usually, the Opry was the place where new talent was discovered. But sometimes, the public came to know an unusual new performer even before he or she got to the Opry. In 1949, for example, Hank Williams made his debut on the program. The audience did not recognize his name when he was introduced onstage. But almost everyone knew who he was the moment he began singing his new song "Lovesick Blues." As he sang, applause washed over the stage like an ocean tide. He sang six encores before master of ceremonies Red Foley finally persuaded the audience to let the rest of the show continue. The occasion made Williams an instant country music star.

Development of the star system brought new prestige to the Grand Ole Opry as well as to its stars. One result was the increased demand for personal appearances by Opry performers. In answer to this demand, the R. J. Reynolds Company, maker of Camel cigarettes and a sponsor of the Opry, organized a tour of Opry stars in 1942. Called the Camel Caravan, it was one of the most significant tours in Opry history. Stars of the Camel Caravan included Pee Wee King, Eddy Arnold, and Minnie Pearl, a commedienne who joined the Opry in 1940. The group played at military bases and hospitals, bringing country music to the attention of many thousands of servicemen who had never heard it before. Later in the 1940s, the Opry sent road shows to such important places as Carnegie Hall in New York.

The new prestige was gratifying to WSM founder Edwin Craig, to Judge Hay, and to others. But they were also concerned. Craig, for one, had never imagined individual performers becoming as famous as the Grand Ole Opry itself. Nor did he feel that the singers presented his beloved country music as accurately as did the string musicians. Hay, too, was forever telling his troupe to "keep it down to earth, boys"—meaning that they should play traditional country music.

But performers were not as concerned about how things had been done in the past. They were more interested in finding new ways to improve their sound and to make their acts more entertaining. The McGee brothers, who were among the pioneer artists at WSM, thought that one way to improve their sound in the late 1930s was to play electric guitars. This was too modern for Hay's tastes, however, and he didn't allow them to do it. But gradually, through the persistence of performers like Pee Wee King, western swing band leader Bob Wills, and Ernest Tubb, electric instruments worked their way onto the Opry stage. During the early 1940s, drums also were adopted.

There were other clashes between artists and management, too. Around 1936, Hay had fired the black harmonica player DeFord Bailey, supposedly for refusing to learn any new songs. It was a different matter, though, trying to dictate to stars who had established reputations. One night, Archie Campbell refused to wear the traditional rural costume, and he walked onstage to perform in his street clothes. Still, not all displays of independence could be tolerated. The Opry refused Eddy Arnold's demand for a percentage of the gate receipts. And Hank Williams was fired in 1951 for missing performances.

A characteristic strength of the Opry, however, was that whenever performers left the show, new talent could always be found to replace them. In the 1950s, when the rock and roll craze swept the music world, most live country music programs folded. And most country radio stations switched to playing rock and roll records. Yet during this decade, the Opry popularized many new stars, including Hank Snow, Marty Robbins, Jim Reeves, Porter Wagoner, Stonewall Jackson, Kitty Wells, Jean Shepard, Roy Drusky, and Patsy Cline.

Kitty Wells

Most of the new performers were brought to the Opry by Jim Denny. Denny had started his career in the mail room of the National Life and Accident Insurance Company in 1927, when he was 16 years old. But the Opry fascinated him more than the insurance company, so he hung around the theater, running errands, answering phones, and ushering at performances. He even worked as a bouncer at the Opry, throwing out troublemakers.

Later, Denny familiarized himself with various aspects of WSM management. These included heading concessions, helping Jack Stapp produce live shows for the network, and working with the Artists Service Bureau. Eventually, Denny was made director of the Bureau, and in 1947 he succeeded Judge Hay as manager of the Opry. The Judge, who was in ill health, had long since given up administrative duties. Denny's promotion merely confirmed officially the fact that he had been one of the powers backstage for some time. As such, he decided who would perform at the Opry, and he booked road appearances for Opry artists.

Ironically, the experience and ability that made Denny so influential and important also led to his downfall. He was branching into areas of broadcasting, songwriting, and publishing outside of WSM. Top management at the station felt that this amounted to a conflict of interest with the Grand Ole Opry. So Denny was fired in 1956, the same year that *Billboard* magazine named him Country Music Man of the Year.

The firing did not hurt Denny, for he became successful in a number of other activities within the Nashville music community. As for the Opry, losing Denny did not stunt its growth either. Development of the star system had greatly expanded the scope of country music. There was plenty of room for both the institution that created the system and for the individuals who profited from it.

In a sense, all who participated were on the same team, working toward a common goal. Together, they would bring new respectability to country music and truly make Nashville "Music City, U.S.A."

Some stars have contributed in a special way to the growth of the Grand Ole Opry and to the development of country music. They have been honored for their contributions by induction into the Country Music Association's Hall of Fame. Their plaques can be seen at the Country Music Hall of Fame Museum in Nashville.

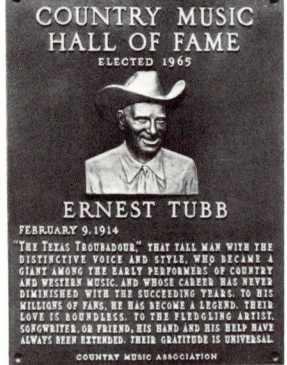

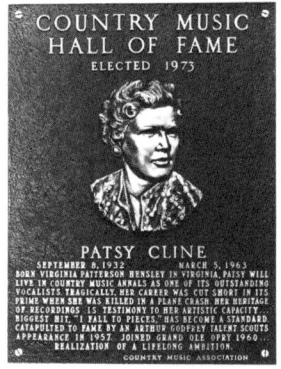

Ryman Auditorium

Home at the Ryman   5

For the first 16 years of its existence, the Grand Ole Opry was like a nomad, wandering from place to place. It had been broadcast from three different locations at WSM Radio and then had moved to the Hillsboro Theater in 1934, to the Dixie Tabernacle in 1936, and finally to the handsome new War Memorial Auditorium in 1939. Before long, however, city officials became unhappy about the wear-and-tear that exuberant Opry fans inflicted on their newly constructed auditorium. So in 1941, the Opry was forced to move again. Its new home became the Ryman Auditorium, on Fifth Street just off Broadway in downtown Nashville.

The Ryman's earthy history made it an appropriate home for country music. Originally named the Union Gospel Tabernacle, the building had been constructed in 1891 by Tom Ryman, a riverboat captain. Captain Ryman's fleet of boats navigated the Cumberland River, which flowed through Nashville. The boats were known to house various illegal activities, so the captain had a questionable reputation.

One night, as a joke, Captain Ryman went to a religious tent meeting. His purpose was to heckle the evangelist preacher, the Reverend Sam Jones. Instead, Ryman was converted by the preacher's spellbinding sermon. So impressed was he by the Reverend Jones' message that he vowed to help save other souls. As a result, Captain Ryman built a tabernacle for the preacher who had so changed his life.

In later years, the building was used for other meetings as well. In 1897, a reunion of Confederate veterans was held there, and a balcony was constructed for the occasion. Later, a stage was added. With these improvements and with a seating capacity of more than 3,000, the tabernacle gradually began to be used more and more as a concert hall and theater. Eventually the name of the building was changed to Ryman Auditorium.

By 1941, when the Grand Ole Opry arrived, many years had passed since the Ryman had been used primarily as a gospel hall. Yet, it still looked like a gospel hall, and that's what it felt like to visitors. The oaken pews and the semicircular seating arrangement automatically drew the attention of the audience to the speaker.

This arrangement fit the Grand Ole Opry perfectly. Performers could easily establish a personal rapport with the fans in such a setting. And this rapport was somehow transmitted over the radio, making the Opry even more enjoyable for the audience at home. As the popularity of each star grew at the Ryman, so did the prestige of the Opry and of its music.

Gradually Ryman Auditorium became more than just a place to have performances. It became a dramatic and solid foundation for a long tradition of good country music. It was as basic to the Opry's success as Judge George Hay's naming of the Opry years before. The Ryman became so much a part of the show that it served as the Grand Ole Opry house for more than 30 years. As time passed, the building got an unofficial symbolic title, too—the "Mother Church of Country Music."

Of course, neither the country music industry nor the Grand Ole Opry grew solely because of the popularity of the Ryman. But the converted gospel temple did lend permanence and stability to the Opry. Among performers and audience members alike, there was a feeling of belonging to a family. And among the people producing the shows, there was an increasing awareness of the potential of country music. A new pride and confidence about the future of the industry began to emerge.

The change in the industry's image became evident in 1943 after Ernest Tubb joined the Opry. He soon decided that he didn't want to be known as a "hillbilly" singer any longer. The term, he thought, had a negative image. Tubb got his recording company, Decca, to list him in its catalog as a "country singer" instead.

The image of country music changed even more with the advent of recording studios in Nashville. Three engineers from station WSM started the first recording studio in Nashville in 1945, and WSM's music director soon opened a second one. Decca and other major recording companies came to town, followed by record processing plants, talent agencies, trade newspapers, and other businesses connected with the music industry. As a result of the rise in Nashville's music-related industries, veteran WSM announcer David Cobb began calling Nashville "Music City." The name stuck, and for good reason. Today there are about 60 recording studios in Nashville, and more than 15,000 recording sessions are held annually.

In 1951, the first annual Grand Ole Opry birthday celebration for country music disc jockeys took place. About 100 people attended. From that small beginning, the celebration has grown into a four-day event attracting more than 6,000 disc jockeys, talent directors, publishers, musicians, record company executives, and others employed in the music industry. A portion of the event's registration fee goes into the Opry Trust Fund, established in 1965 to aid country musicians and families in distress. So far, about $300,000 has been distributed.

The initial gathering of disc jockeys in 1951 inspired them to form their own association three years later. This led to the formation of the Country Music Association (CMA) in 1958, an effective trade organization that has done much to promote country music. One event sponsored by the CMA, the Grand Ole Opry, and station WSM is the International Country Music Fan Fair in

Bill Monroe and his band performing at the Fan Fair in 1977

June. The Fan Fair is attended by more than 15,000 fans, who come from all 50 states, and foreign countries as well.

In the 1950s, the country music industry and the Opry turned their sights toward television, and with good results. WSM, Nashville's first television station, achieved the same quality of excellence with television shows as it had with the live radio shows in the 1930s. The live TV shows became so popular that segments of the Opry were shown on network television programs. And Opry stars such as Porter Wagoner, Del Reeves, Jim Ed Brown, and Bill Anderson got their own syndicated TV shows, which were filmed onstage at the Ryman.

By the mid-1960s, country music was an established nationwide industry. The Opry, too, was expanding. Ott Devine, the manager of the Opry, added a Friday night show to accommodate the growing crowds. Talented new stars such as Loretta Lynn, Dolly Parton, Jack Greene, Jeannie Seely, and the Osborne brothers joined the Opry roster.

Modern times, however, brought a new problem. Executives of the National Life and Accident Insurance Company and of station WSM were concerned about the ancient Ryman. National Life, through a subsidiary, owned the building, which it had acquired from the city of Nashville in 1964. The company had been trying to keep the Ryman as up-to-date as possible, but there were still problems. Entry ways and exits were inadequate; the building was not air-conditioned; the hard, wooden seats were uncomfortable; and there were no parking facilities. It was clearly time to consider another home for the Grand Ole Opry.

E. W. ("Bud") Wendell, who had become the new Opry manager, suggested that the next home of the Grand Ole Opry be more than just a new Opry house. He wanted it to be part of a musical showplace, a family entertainment park where people could hear all kinds of American music. In 1969 National Life decided to take a big gamble and build "Opryland U.S.A.," a 358-acre park about nine miles northeast of downtown Nashville.

Original plans called for the Ryman Auditorium to be demolished when the new Opry house at Opryland was ready, but this aroused a storm of protest. To country music fans, tearing down the Ryman would be like tearing down a shrine. So the Ryman still stands, and it has become one of the most nostalgic and popular stops for tourists in Nashville. Many of them are almost overwhelmed when they stand on the stage where so many of their favorites performed for so many years.

The last show at Ryman Auditorium was held on Friday, March 15, 1974. For several months before that, Opry management had waged a public relations campaign designed to promote the place the Opry was going to rather than the building it was

The last show at the Ryman

leaving. The stars generally cooperated in interviews by playing down their feelings and affection for the Ryman.

Nonetheless, that last show was an emotional scene, heightened by the presence of a number of reporters and photographers who wanted to record the historic departure. Some of the stars were unable to maintain their casual air. Minnie Pearl, the queen of country comedy whose career had blossomed on the stage of the Ryman, broke up when the crowd gave her a standing ovation. The usually calm Bill Anderson became so nervous he forgot his lyrics. Another singer, Jean Shepard, confessed to having "very mixed emotions," struggled through two numbers, and then dashed offstage in tears.

An era had come to an end. As Shepard said, "I can't pretend that this isn't special. I can't pretend it doesn't hurt to leave."

Live entertainment is featured at Opryland U.S.A.

The Opry Today   6

Opryland U.S.A. is a lively, fun-filled entertainment and recreation park where music is always in the air. The park is divided into towns or areas based on different musical styles, such as jazz, folk, country, and rock-and-roll. Because Opryland's basic concept is to provide live, natural, and authentic entertainment, visitors will find no animation or aspects of fantasy there.

The feeling of authenticity that visitors to Opryland get is provided by well-constructed settings and costumes from different periods in American history. The attractive settings are enhanced by a natural backdrop of trees, flowers, and shrubs that dot the adjacent hills and walking paths. At certain points along the paths, there are even "people cages" to protect human visitors from the deer, cougar, bears, and timber wolves that roam the hills. For humans who are interested in something a little less wild, there are rides adapted from the past. Among the most popular is the "Flume Zoom," which carries passengers in hollowed-out logs.

The cost of constructing Opryland to date is $46 million, of which $15 million was used to build the Opry house. This total is much higher than the original estimate made in the late 1960s, and there is still land left to be developed. If the National Life and Accident Company executives had known that the complex would cost so much, they might

One of many exciting rides at Opryland

never have gone ahead with plans for Opryland. But even without a park, a new Opry house would have been built anyway, because the insurance company executives felt that the Opry should keep up with the times.

The designers of the new Opry house tried to put the best of the old and the new into their plans. Their design represented an effort to keep the earthy, warm character that made the Ryman so popular, while building up the Opry's prestige in a highly competitive entertainment world. Keeping some of the Ryman's warmth was no small feat. The old Opry house's appeal stemmed from the informality and intimacy of its tabernacle layout, which preserved the closeness between audience members, and between audience and performer. But how could this relationship be preserved in the new Opry house with its intended 4,400 seats?

Faced with that challenge, the architects attempted to design a building that would win fans over at first sight. The exterior of the building is made of materials that give a warm, friendly impression. Brick and rustic wood panels help convey that idea. The roof has a shake shingle look, and the eaves overhang the front and sides to form a porch-like entrance.

The lobby, built of rustic wood paneling and brick, has a high slanted wood-beamed ceiling and heavy timber stair railings. The air-conditioned auditorium is furnished with pew-like benches that resemble those at the Ryman, but that are far more comfortable with their padded seats and contoured backs. The closeness between family members and friends has, therefore, been preserved.

Closeness between performer and audience has also been preserved. There is much more standing room in front of the stage at the new Opry house than at the Ryman, so that fans can come up and snap pictures of their favorite stars anytime — something the Opry staff encourages them to do.

The exterior of the new Grand Ole Opry house

Even the balcony, which wraps part way around the stage, gives the audience sitting there a sense of closeness to the stars. And vision on both floors is unobstructed, unlike the old Ryman, where pillars blocked the view for part of the audience.

As large and plush as the new auditorium is, the people in the audience are always aware that they are in a broadcasting studio (which happens to be the world's largest). The traditional painted backdrops promoting sponsors' products are part of the show, just as they were at the Ryman. Also visible

Inside the new Opry house

is a space frame, a sort of platform suspended above the stage that contains lights, catwalks, speaker horns, and other equipment. This further reminds Opry fans that they are watching a live performance that is being broadcast to millions. Just as in the old days, the audience's excitement is transmitted to the audience at home, which helps make a good show.

The new Opry house was designed with the performer in mind, too. It has the latest in sound and electronic equipment, enabling the soloist and the accompanist to hear each other better. Backstage are 12 dressing rooms, a makeup room, a kitchenette, a band rehearsal room, and a lounge. A separate, 300-seat television production center is also located behind the stage. It is equipped for videotaping or televising network or nationally syndicated shows. WSM-TV staff, Opryland officials, and network and independent producers all use this center.

One Opry brochure points out that "no expenses were spared" in constructing the Grand Ole Opry house and Opryland. The total cost of the project is enough to make some National Life executives wince even now. But National Life's gamble *has* paid off. Both Opryland and the Opry have proven profitable. Opryland draws about two million people annually. Admission is $6.50 for adults and $5 for children. Additional money comes from restaurants and gift shops.

Opry performances are similarly successful. They are sold out weeks, and sometimes months, in advance, even though the new Opry house has about 1,300 more seats than the Ryman. Seats to the Opry cost $5 for reserved and $3 for general admission. The Friday night Opry runs 8 to 11, and two shows are held on Saturday night, from 6:30 to 9 and from 9:30 to midnight. To take care of overflow crowds, the Opry also holds a two-hour Saturday matinee during the summer.

Any profit coming from the Opry house itself is considered a bonus by the National Life executives. The program would continue even if it were not making money, because it is a door opener for the insurance sales representatives, just as Edwin Craig predicted that it would be years ago. No one can say with certainty how much insurance business results from the company's association with the Opry, but the sales people themselves are quick to point out that the value is substantial.

The Opry's newness and profit-making capacity does trouble some performers though. They have nagging doubts precisely because the Opry has become "big business." They are afraid that the program may have lost its soul when it left the Ryman Auditorium. They think that fans react differently in the luxurious $15 million studio-auditorium than they used to in the old tabernacle.

But if the Grand Ole Opry house does not have quite the same "down-home" feeling that the Ryman had, neither are the fans all down-home folks anymore. They are generally more sophisticated, and they like many different kinds of country music. In spite of the slight opposition to the new Opry house, the Opry is still giving a lot of people what they want to hear.

While most fans are happy with the Opry's new image, traditional down-to-earth singers such as Roy Acuff, Skeeter Davis, and Stoney Cooper are sometimes uneasy about it. There is a trend, they feel, away from authentic country music. Others who have been with the Opry for a long time think that it no longer has a comfortable family atmosphere. They feel that the performers appear to be having less fun and that they do not seem to be mixing as well with each other or with the fans.

Among some of the artists, there is another source of tension. Opry artists are required by contract to perform 20 weekends out of the year. They are paid $120 for playing the Saturday night Opry and $60 for all other shows. That doesn't seem like very much to them when they hear how much was spent on the new building or how profitable the Opry is. Any performer who is reasonably popular can make 20 times that amount playing a date on the road. On the other hand, the Opry is helpful in giving a performer exposure, so that he or she can command good fees on the road.

   Big stars such as Johnny Cash, Merle Haggard, and Glen Campbell are not members of the Grand Ole Opry. But the fact that artists can have a successful career without the Opry does not mean that the program is unimportant. It simply means that the country music industry and especially the Grand Ole Opry are continually changing, making way for new artists all the time. The Opry is a place for beginning and experienced artists alike to learn and to grow.

Tex Ritter and Vito Pellettieri at the Opry

Opry Tradition   7

It was Saturday night at the Grand Ole Opry House. The backstage door used by performers and Opry staff opened to reveal an elderly white-haired man in a wheelchair. He was being pushed by his attendant, and a nurse accompanied them.

The old man exchanged greetings with the guard at the desk, his ancient eyes twinkling behind his glasses. Then the attendant wheeled the old man down a long corridor leading to the stage of the Grand Ole Opry. Soon he was on stage, smiling, looking back and forth, and waiting eagerly for something to happen.

The man was Vito Pellettieri, who for nearly 40 years had been the energetic, firm-handed, no-nonsense stage manager of the Grand Ole Opry. He had kidded with, worried about, and at times bawled out everyone from Roy Acuff to Charley Pride. Once a nervous Faron Young, making his debut at the Opry, started on stage before getting the proper cue. Pellettieri almost knocked him down. "You just watch me, boy," he admonished. "I'll tell you when it's time."

Even when Pellettieri was in his mid-80s and in failing health, he held onto his burning interest in show business. His wife had died a few years before, so he was living in a nursing home. But every Saturday night, an attendant and a nurse would bring Vito back to the Grand Ole Opry, which was as special to him as grandchildren are to grandparents.

The show began as usual on this particular Saturday night. But it was to take place in surroundings far different from those that Vito had known in his years with the Opry. This was the new Grand Ole Opry house. The stage was bigger—110 feet wide and 68 feet deep. There were more people in the audience, and many of the seats were farther away from the stage than at the old Ryman.

But much about the Opry was the same, too. During the show, people milled about on stage in plain view of the audience, while a few yards in front of them a performer was singing into a microphone. Flash bulbs popped in front of the stage. And an assistant producer checked notes in answer to questions about who was supposed to go on next. When a performer finished a number, the master of ceremonies would wave his hand in a silent urge for applause. Periodically the entertainment was stopped while an announcer read a commercial. Behind him, backdrops went up and down, depending on which company was sponsoring that part of the program. And there was always a never-ending procession of back-up bands setting up equipment or taking it down.

Vito Pellettieri sat in his wheelchair that evening, absorbing everything, sometimes nodding and sometimes frowning. A dozen or so featured artists from the Opry's regular roster of about 60 performers trooped on and off the stage. There were old-timers from the 30s, 40s, and 50s such as Roy Acuff, Ernest Tubb, Wilma Lee and Stoney Cooper, Lester Flatt, and Stonewall Jackson. And there were younger people — Bill Anderson, Dottie West, and Connie Smith.

The performers responded to Vito with respect. Young or old, each person stopped to talk and joke with him, as if greeting him were part of the Grand Ole Opry tradition. The women usually bent down to kiss him. Vito always looked like a man who expected such treatment.

In a way, the respect paid to Vito was part of Opry tradition. Certainly Vito Pellettieri was not on stage that evening to provide any real direction. It was no longer his job to bark out commands and keep the show moving. But his very presence linked the past with the present. He represented stability to the older artists, and wisdom and experience to the younger artists. When Vito died in 1977, some of the Opry's ties with the past died with him.

The younger generation, however, will have to make use of Vito's wisdom and experience in its own way. The future strength of the Grand Ole Opry lies in the realization by the new generation that it is carrying on the work of such great men as Edwin Craig, George D. Hay, and Vito Pellettieri.

Opposite page: The Country Music Association has recognized the contributions of all different kinds of people in the field of entertainment. Outstanding individuals in the broadcasting and recording industries (as well as performers) have been inducted into the Hall of Fame. Their plaques hang beside those of the stars in the Country Music Hall of Fame in Nashville.

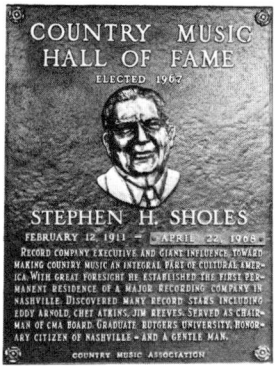

Index

Acuff-Rose Publications, 36
Acuff, Roy, 35-36
Arnold, Eddy, 38
Artists' Service Bureau, 32
"Athens of the South," Nashville as, 12

Bailey, DeFord, 23, 40
barn dance programs, 9, 10, 21
bluegrass music, 38

Camel Caravan (Opry tour), 39
Country Music Association (CMA), 51
Craig, C. A., 10, 14
Craig, Edwin W., 10-11, 13-14, 15, 16, 28, 30, 39

Denny, Jim, 42-43

Foley, Red, 38

Hay, George D., 14, 15-17, 18, 21, 23, 30, 35, 39, 40, 42
hillbilly music, 9, 10, 50
honky tonk singing, 37
International Country Music Fan Fair, 51-52

Macon, Uncle Dave, 20-21, 35
Monroe, Bill, 38
"Musical Appreciation Hour," 21
"Music City U.S.A.," Nashville as, 5-7, 43, 50. *See also* Nashville, Tennessee
music industry, 49-50, 65

Nashville, Tennessee, 5, 11-13
"National Barn Dance" (Radio WLS), 10, 15, 16
National Life and Accident Insurance Company, 10-11, 14, 28, 52

Opryland U.S.A., 53, 57-64

Pellettieri, Vito, 31-32, 67-70

radio, importance of, 10, 18
Radio WSM, 13-14, 16, 25-26, 33
records, importance of, 10
Reynolds Company, 33, 39
Rose, Fred, 36
Ryman Auditorium, 47-49, 52-55

"Solemn Old Judge." *See* Hay, George D.
Stapp, Jack, 33
"star system," development of, 43
Stone, Harry, 30

talent scouts, 10
Thompson, Uncle Jimmy, 17-18
Tubb, Ernest, 37, 50

Williams, Hank, 38-39
WSM "Barn Dance," 23

WITHDRAWN

VERMONT DEPT. OF LIBRARIES
0 00 01 0338024 2